C000076862

LIGHT a CaNDLe

reflections &prayers
for our time

Pauline
BOOKS & MEDIA

First published in the United Kingdom in 2021

Pauline Books & Media
84 Church Street, Liverpool L1 3AY
© 2021 Pauline Books & Media UK

ISBN 9781904785804

Photography and graphic design, Mary Louise Winters fsp

Pauline Books & Media wish to acknowledge and thank
Patrick, Daniel and Brendan Boyd, Keira Dowds and Olivia Millar
who contributed the prayers on page 74.

Pauline

BOOKS & MEDIA
www.PaulineUK.org
email: orders@pauline-uk.org

Pauline Books & Media is an expression of the ministry of the Daughters of St Paul,
an international Catholic community of religious women,
dedicated to spreading the Good News of Jesus Christ, using all media in the spirit of the Apostle Paul.

a candle is lit

The use of candles
as part of a prayerful meditation
is powerful.

Children and adults respond
to the quieting effect that a candle flame brings.

Each of these reflections opens up
a whole area of wondering and engagement
that can be a creative stimulus for prayer.

a candle is lit.........

Archbishop John Wilson

for our churches

We know the Church is more than a building.
But our churches and chapels are part of our lives.
We gather there to worship and celebrate.
The rhythm of our lives, and of each year,
is marked and mapped in our churches.

Of course, we can pray at home.
We can pray anywhere.
But our church is familiar, our spiritual home.
How different the landscape would be without churches.
How different our lifescape would be if they were absent.

For all that happens in and through our churches,
for the prayer and praise within,
for the service that flows out,
let us light a candle of gratitude.

WHERE TWO
OR THREE
GATHER
IN MY NAME
I AM THERE
WITH
THEM

Matthew 18:20

Lord Jesus,

the Church is your body,
with each of us its precious members.

Renew the communities of faith
which gather in our churches.

Renew the life of worship and prayer,
and of justice and charity that reach beyond the walls.

Bless those who founded,
funded and built our places of worship.

May we never take them for granted,
but, ever open to the Holy Spirit,
ensure they serve your love for the world.

Amen

a candle is lit·········

for leaders

A leader is only a leader when they have followers.

Very often we confuse leadership with power.
No one becomes an effective leader
because they have been given a title,
a position, or power.

A good leader goes first, is prepared to be in a vulnerable
position and takes the risk before asking others to follow.

A good leader lives a life of integrity, is compassionate and
makes sacrifices for their followers.

Jesus is the true leader.
He did not have position, power or title,
yet he walked the journey
and people were inspired to follow;
and by allowing himself to become vulnerable
he became strong.
By embracing death, he offers life to all.

I AM AMONG YOU AS ONE WHO serves...

Luke 22:27

Lord Jesus,

we bring before you all those who lead and guide us.
We ask you to bless those who lead us in our families,
schools, churches, our places of work and all organisations
that impact our lives. We pray also for those who make
decisions in leading our country and countries across the
world.

As we light this candle, we are reminded of the light you
brought into the lives of all people who encountered you
in the Gospels and down through the ages, dispelling
darkness and giving life. May today's leaders follow your
example and put their followers first. May they act with
integrity and always be courageous and compassionate.

May they use their energy building your Kingdom:
a kingdom of Justice, Love and Peace. May your light bring
hope and peace into our world and shatter darkness
wherever it may be, allowing your love
to be encountered by all.
We ask this in your most powerful name, Lord Jesus.

Amen

a candle is lit ·········

Victoria Battell

for health carers

The tender touch, a word of compassion,
a reassuring look, a hand held:
these are the moments in time which provide
hope to those who are vulnerable and anxious.

When loved ones cannot be present,
healthcare providers reassure,
often at their own risk and away from their own families.

To lay down one's life for one's friends,
is the example of Jesus,
and the witness to Christ by care providers.
They are the light of Christ giving hope in dark times.

No work of mercy escapes these kind people;
they welcome the stranger, feed the hungry,
and take care of the sick.
They have ministered
to the least of Jesus' brothers and sisters.
They have been his hands, his feet, and his love.

JUST AS YOU DID IT TO ONE OF THE LEAST OF THESE WHO ARE MEMBERS OF MY FAMILY YOU DID IT

Matthew 25:40

TO ME

Loving Jesus,

place your healing hand on all who are sick
and those who care for them.

May we know your presence at this time.

Be with all who are lonely
and have no one to care for them.

Be with those who are afraid
and in need of peace.

With gratitude,
we pray for all those who care for others,
and who use their skills to restore us to health.

May their tireless efforts be rewarded
by your grace,
in this life and the next.

Amen

for frontline workers

The dark storm of these times exposed our vulnerability,
the flimsiness of human certainties we built up
to imagine we were in control.
Now a silver lining emerges allowing us time
for choosing what really matters and what fades away.
Those we saw rise up in our midst
going out onto the front lines to serve us
have shown us a new way.
Though anxious for themselves and their families,
they overcame fear to keep our communities going.
Before the storm they were forgotten people –
in the background –
who now have become the fabric of our society;
carers and cleaners, blue light services and transportation,
shops, schools and transport.
They chose to serve rather than panic,
to make adjustments and take responsibility,
and so have written a decisive chapter
in a time of real darkness.

THE DAYS OF
a GOOD LIFE
are NUMBERED
BUT
a GOOD NAME
LASTS FOR ever
BE TRUE TO YOUR TRAINING
AND BE AT PEACE

Sirach 41:13

Lord Jesus,

you do nothing in vain
and in your providence you have allowed us this time
for judging what really matters,
what is of true value.

In this endeavour,
help us to draw lessons from the many people
who – even afraid –
responded by risking themselves in service of the needy.

And so showed us the power of the Spirit
in courageous and generous self-giving.

Amen

23

a candle is lit ○○○○○○○○○○○

for those who have died

As time passes we recall our loved ones
who have gone before us marked with the sign of faith.
We treasure their memory.

We feel their gentle presence comforting us.
We hear the quiet whisper of their voice deep inside,
encouraging us to enjoy the beauty and goodness of life.

A sense of peace gently pours over us,
knowing they are now with God.

Those whom we have loved and lost
continue to inspire and help us to embrace each moment
with gratitude and faith.

We await the day when we will be reunited in life eternal.

Holy Mary, Mother of God,
pray for us at the hour of our death.

THOSE WHOM WE LOVE AND LOSE

are no longer WHERE THEY WERE BEFORE

THEY are NOW WHEREVER WE are

St John Chrysostom

Lord Jesus,

in the light of this candle
we treasure memories held
in the sacred chamber of our hearts.
We quietly recall – with gratitude –
the blessing they have been in our lives.

As we remember we smile, laugh,
look back on the regrets and *if onlys,*
allowing the silent tears shed to heal us.
With gratitude to you, Lord Jesus,
we recall how their precious qualities
and faith have shaped us.

Thank you for the gift of their lives
and the life we shared.

Amen

a CANDLE IS LIT·········

Carole O'Connor

for those who grieve

There is such pain in the goodbye,
so much longing in the waiting for the day
when we will reunite.

Grief wraps itself around us.
We are confused,
no longer sure of where you are.
Yet we lean on you and we are given strength.

You know the pain of leaving loved ones.
Our cries of 'where are you, Lord?' do not fall on deaf ears.

For you are there by our side,
giving comfort, attentive, always loving.

MY PEACE
I GIVE TO YOU

DO NOT LET YOUR HEARTS BE TROUBLED

John 14:27

Lord Jesus,

today we walk through the valley of darkness
with you as our only light.

You, too, wept when you heard your friend had died
and know our pain and anguish.

Fill us with your love and light –
allow us to be open to your
promise of resurrection;
that one day we will be where you are,
reunited with those who have gone before us
and finally contemplating you
face to face for all eternity.

Amen

a CANDLE IS LIT·········

for those
who are exploited

To be exploited means being taken for granted.

A person's gifts and efforts, their very life is made use of,
traded with, consumed, but given no respect or value.

God speaks powerfully through the prophets:
'Let justice roll down like waters,
and righteousness like a mighty stream!'

Justice shines a light in dark places,
acknowledges the true worth of each precious life.

Each of us is a pearl of great price in God's eyes,
a treasure hidden in a field that God's love will uncover.

MAY YOUR STEADFAST

LOVE

BE UPON US

O LORD

as we
PLACE ALL OUR

HOPE

IN YOU

Psalm 33:22

Lord Jesus,

you proclaim a kingdom of righteousness.

Where the labour of the poor is exploited,
may your abundant generosity overflow.

Where the bodies of your beautiful children
are consumed and abused,
may you bathe them in the light of your dignity.

Where the giftedness of each unique person is ignored,
may they find their full value
in the light of your loving gaze.

Amen

a canDLe is LiT·········

for the refugees

Their dignity has been torn from them.

They see no future for themselves and their children.

They are in a dark place
and they need the light

of love
and hope

to guide them through their darkness.

OUT OF THE
DEPTHS
I cry
to you
O LORD
HEAR MY VOICE!

Lord Jesus,

help us to light a way to security and well-being
for these your people
fleeing their homeland
in the hope of a better future.

In the light of this candle,
may we never lose sight of them.

In the light of this candle,
may they never lose sight of you.

Amen

a CANDLE IS LIT·········

for hope

To need hope means that something is beyond us.

It is a cry born from the very centre of our being:
a reaching out to a Greater Other – God.

It is an answer to that which threatens our existence.

Can hope be about today and now,
and not just an antidote to a fearful tomorrow?

To hope is to light a candle within us.

It is to fall at the feet of Jesus in our brokenness;
to admit that we know we're not in control.

Hope is a prayer that all will be well;
that God has us safe in his hands.

HOPE DOES NOT DISAPPOINT

BECAUSE GOD'S LOVE HAS BEEN POURED INTO OUR HEARTS

Romans 5:5

Lord Jesus,

take over, take control!

Let us see your resurrected life in this difficult situation.

Bring life where there is despair,
bring joy where there is fear.

Bring comfort where there is loneliness.

Protect those whom we love
and bless them with the gift of Hope
that you may always be glorified in our lives.

Amen

a candle is lit··········

Fr Michael Campion

for those in darkness

Sometimes in darkness, when no quick solution is in sight,
we might plead to God for our worst fears not to be realised.

Jesus did likewise in the Garden of Gethsemane
on the night he was arrested (Mark 14:32-42).

Feeling alone and terrified,
he begged God to spare him his fate,
just as we might do.

Eventually, over the dark and agonising night,
Jesus understood what God was asking
and was given the strength to accept it,
painful though it would be.

LORD GOD OF MY SALVATION

WHEN AT NIGHT I CRY OUT IN YOUR PRESENCE

LET MY PRAYER COME BEFORE YOU

INCLINE YOUR EAR TO MY CRY

Psalm 88: 1-2

Lord Jesus,

grant comfort to those who are in difficult situations,
especially when there is no solution.

Bring light to their darkness,
strengthen them in their weakness,
take away all fear
and give them your peace.

a CANDLE IS LIT·········

48

Claire Howell

for renewed courage

Courage is in finding the strength
to do something or face a situation
which frightens us.

When life is overwhelming or the future uncertain,
when faced with grief or pain
when every fibre of our being tells us
to run and hide from the world,
to shut everything out and not face reality.

To find courage is to light a candle within us.

It is to run into the arms of Jesus,
to allow ourselves to cry that we are afraid,
to acknowledge our fear, our pain, our anxiety, our distress,
and hand it over to the One who loves us –
to trust in his words,
'Do not be afraid.'

DO NOT BE ANXIOUS YOU SHALL REJOICE AND HAVE ABUNDANCE

2 Esdras 2:27

Lord Jesus,

I trust in you!

Let me feel your protective love envelope me
and your perfect love rid me of my fear,
as I find strength in you.

I know you will never leave me or forsake me,
but will draw close to me as I find the courage I need,
and remain with me wherever I go.

Amen

a CANDLE IS LIT.........

Fr David Wallace

for families

Family is belonging – a belonging that changes with time.

Family is the joy of new life and the burden of grief.

Family is where we treasure togetherness and tenderness.

Family is also where we know the pain of separations.

Where do we experience the reality of family life?

In the struggles of finding a place for a child to be born;
in the anxiety of parents losing their child in the temple;
in the journey made by a mother
whose Son is condemned to death.

And so much more.

FAITH GROWS
WHEN IT IS LIVED
AND SHAPED
Pope Francis
BY LOVE

54

Lord Jesus,

in lighting a candle,
we pray for our families.

We belong together, we can be strong together.

In the joys and the sorrows of our lives,
our families are where we recognise the presence of God.
Living Lord, we recall the example of your family,
a family modelling love and togetherness
to give us an example to follow.

In the joys and sorrows of our family life,
we look to you for guidance, strength and hope.

Keep us always in your love
as we journey together in faith through this life
and bring us home one day to be with you forever
in the place you have prepared for us
in the kingdom of heaven.

Amen

a candle is lit………

for schools

Pope Francis said,
education cannot be neutral.

It is either positive or negative;
either it enriches or it impoverishes;
either it enables a person to grow or it lessens,
even corrupts them.

The mission of schools is to develop a sense of truth,
of what is good and beautiful.

And this occurs through a rich path
made up of many ingredients.

This is why there are so many subjects -
because development is the result of different elements
that act together and stimulate intelligence, knowledge,
the emotions, the body, and so on.

LET THE LITTLE CHILDREN COME TO ME THE KINGDOM OF HEAVEN BELONGS TO THESE

Matthew 19:14

Loving Father,

we place our schools in your hands.

Strengthen them in their mission
of leading pupils to a personal encounter with Christ.

May our schools shine as beacons,
bringing light to children and young people,
their families and the parishes they serve.

Inspire school leaders and staff
to develop and share a curriculum
which glorifies Your name,
so that their pupils can grow in holiness,
 knowledge and appreciation
of all that is true and good and beautiful.

We ask this in Your Son's name.

Amen

a candle is lit·········

for the lonely

Loneliness is part of the human experience.

It can be painful and cause us to fear, to suffer.

Surrender to the loneliness,
the abyss of empty dreams.

Embrace Absence
for within it there is Presence
– presence of the Lord of all,
your Lord, who whispers
'I am here.'

– A God whose love surrounds and penetrates.
In God is our homeland.

THE LORD IS NEAR TO ALL WHO CALL ON HIM

Psalm 145:18

Lord Jesus,

in our time spent alone
may we remain in loving awareness of your presence.

For those moments,
when alone or in company,
when we experience deep loneliness,
console us,
bless and strengthen us, loving Lord.

Your heart envelops all who suffer.

We ask this, Lord Jesus,
for ourselves,
for those who feel lonely this day,
for those who feel lonely this night.

Amen

a candle is lit·········

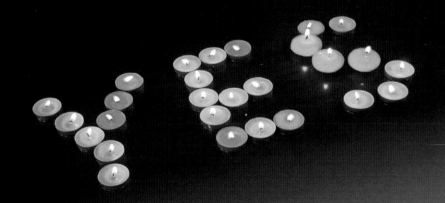

for vocations

It is hard to believe and accept that every one of us, including me, is called to holiness – to be holy as God is holy.
The universal call to holiness is our fundamental vocation, and every living person is worthy of that call.

If we wish to hear God then we must listen, but what is it that gets in the way of hearing God's voice, his call?
We know why our ears are stopped: we are too busy for God or we are concerned with our own affairs
or maybe we simply do not know God's voice.

We must listen hard. The voice of God can be heard in the Scriptures, experienced in the Church, in our families,
and it can always be heard in the cry of the poor.
Do we listen out for God in these places?

Light a candle in the place deep within our being so that we may be enlightened by the voice of God speaking to us.
Within our call to holiness, we are called to specific tasks, to give of ourselves, and to speak out for the voiceless.

Are we listening? Am I listening?

DEEP WITHIN OUR BEING

THE VOICE OF GOD IS SPEAKING TO US

Archbishop Malcolm McMahon

Heavenly Father,

open the ears of your faithful people
so that they may hear your voice.

Fill them with your Holy Spirit,
so that they may discern your will for them,
and that they may have the courage to announce
the Good News of your Son's resurrection
wherever you may place them.

We make this prayer through that same Son,
Jesus Christ.

Amen

a candle is lit·········

for Life

Patricia Carol

Life is a precious gift to us all.

It's a spark of God's own life in us.

Its beginnings are fragile and small.

God within us blossoms every day.

From our beginning to our final end God is with us and in us.

To light a candle for life
is to honour the wonder and mystery of our human being.

We are precious to Him at every stage of life.
We can see this in the wonder and fun of the young,
        in the fragile hands of the elderly,
        in hands that reach out in peace,
        in the faces of those who cry out for justice…

I CAME

THAT THEY MAY HAVE

LIFE

AND HAVE IT

ABUNDANTLY

John 10:10

Loving God,

help us to honour life in all its stages.

Give us the grace to value the one precious life we are given.

Help us to support those who are struggling
for human dignity.

May we work to make our world
a place where the dignity of every
woman, man and child
is treasured and upheld.

Amen.

a candle is lit·········

for the media

The internet, digital reporting
and social media present great opportunities
if used responsibly.

Thanks to the internet we have the opportunity
to report what we see, and to share it with others.

At the same time,
the risk of misinformation being spread
has become evident to everyone.
News and images can be easily manipulated,
for any number of reasons.

Being critical in this regard
is not about demonizing the internet,
but rather an incentive to discernment
and responsibility.
All of us are responsible for the information we share.
All of us are to be witnesses of the truth.

World Communications Day is celebrated annually the Sunday before Pentecost.

MAY YOU BE PRAISED LORD GOD

.........for facetime to see my grandparents and my family......

..........for my ipad to play games with my friends online.........

.........for my phone so I can call and message my friends........

.........for internet and social media
so I can stay connected with people......

.........for snapchat to chat and send photos to my friends....

.........for teams so I can tune in for my home learning........

.........for zoom for my hobbies like dancing..............

— Quotes from children aged 6–10 —

Lord Jesus,

we celebrate the writers,
artists, composers, directors,
and all those whose gifts
promote truth and values through media.

May you be praised,
Lord God, for the printed word,
radio, cinema, television, the internet,
digital and social media
which links people around the globe
in solidarity of faith, hope, and love.

Adapted from
The Canticle of Praise for the Media
Blessed Alberione

a candle is lit·········

for our planet

Pope Francis reminds us, throughout *Laudato Si'*,
of our moral obligation to care for our common home,
Mother Earth.
It is about seeing, knowing, sensing, touching and
tasting the sacredness of all life. Like Moses,
we are called to stand before the burning bush,[1]
take a long loving look at the reality before us,
and bow in recognition that we are on Holy Ground.

This awareness invites us to live from a contemplative
perspective – mindful in our activity and from the depths,
to be sensually aware so as to respond with the fullness
of our being.

To live from a contemplative perspective is to experience
something that has existed from the very beginning:[2]
the sacred mystery that we are intrinsically part of – that
we may experience for ourselves,[3] in our own being and in
all of life: the Word made flesh and dwelling,
not only amongst us, but within us.[4]

1. Ex 3: 1-5;   2. 1 Jn 1:1;   3. 1 Jn 1:2;   4. Jn 1:14

THE PLACE ON WHICH YOU are STANDING IS HOLY GROUND

Exodus 3:5

Holy Mystery,

Word made flesh,
grace us with considerate hearts
that will enable us to live and move upon this planet
mindful of the sacredness of all life.

May we,
in recognising your Word made flesh in us,
treat ourselves,
one another
and all creation,
with the same reverence and consideration
with which you embrace all that is.

Amen

a CaNDLe IS LIT · · · · · · · · ·

Accept
this Easter candle.

May it
always dispel
the
darkness
of the
night...

for all

Let me tell you the story of this candle.
We had our largest group of candidates for baptism
and reception into the Church at Easter.
The whole community was filled with joyful excitement.
Everyone was involved. We commissioned an artist
to make us the biggest and most beautiful Easter candle.

And then Covid struck.
We were closed and we were gutted.
We had to abandon our plans and delay our celebration.
I could not bear to celebrate the Easter Vigil on my own
with no parish family. Our beautiful candle went into
the box and was stored away. Then began the long hard
slog of lockdown and restrictions and we were almost
forced apart from each other.
Some days it was all so draining that all I could do
at the end of yet another groundhog, routine day
was to light a little candle in my room …
and remember.

I AM THE LIGHT OF THE WORLD WHOEVER FOLLOWS ME WILL HAVE THE LIGHT OF LIFE

John 8:12

Lord Jesus,

we pray for new life, full of hope and expectation.
We pray also for the sick, the dying, the grieving.

Lord, comfort the elderly, the isolated, the displaced,
who cannot hug their loved ones
and for all distressed families as well.

We remember those who have lost their jobs,
those anxious about money, bills, shelter and food.

We pray for the happy, the healthy,
those who have the means to serve you in their neighbour.

We pray for our many refugees and asylum seekers,
already disorientated – now even more so.

We pray for all your people whose needs only you alone know.

With our prayer,
we light a little flickering candle to burn for them.

Amen